Vermeer's Light

Vermeer's Light

Poems 1996–2006

George Bowering

Talonbooks

Vancouver

Talonbooks
P.O. Box 2076, Vancouver, British Columbia, Canada V6B 3S3
www.talonbooks.com

Typeset in Adobe Garamond and printed and bound in Canada.
Printed on 100% post-consumer recycled paper.

First Revised Printing: February 2007

The publisher gratefully acknowledges the financial support of the Canada Council for the Arts; the Government of Canada through the Book Publishing Industry Development Program; and the Province of British Columbia through the British Columbia Arts Council for our publishing activities.

Library and Archives Canada Cataloguing in Publication

Bowering, George, 1935–
    Vermeer's light : poems, 1996-2006 / George Bowering.

ISBN 0-88922-546-X (bound).—ISBN 978-0-88922-565-7 (pbk.)

    I. Title.

PS8503.O875V47 2006   C811'.54   C2006-902201-1

This book is for my sweetheart, Jean Baird.

Contents

Preface

These poems were written during a time that brought a lot of changes to my life. In the late nineties my wife Angela, who was already living with multiple sclerosis, got cancer and went through three years of operations before dying in the fall of 1999. We had been married for thirty-seven years.

In the fall of 2001 I retired from my job and settled into a life of reading and writing and watching baseball games.

In late 2002 the Canadian Parliament made me the poet laureate, so my settling was over. After a year of crisscrossing the country, I sold the house I had been living in for thirty years and moved to Port Colborne, Ontario for the second half of my laureateship, taking up lodging at the home of Ms. Jean Baird, and travelling once a week to London, Ontario, where I was writer in residence at the University of Western Ontario. I spent most of my time back east in a wheelchair or on crutches, having broken my hip, the way old folks are wont to do. In the summer of 2004 I induced Ms. Baird to come to Vancouver with me and take up residence among the mossy trees. It is kind of a stupid place for a baseball fan to live, but we do get out on the road every summer.

"Sitting in Vancouver" is a sequence I wrote in the late twentieth century, and responds to my 1964 sequence "Sitting in Mexico."

"A, You're Adorable" was written by Ellen Field, a writing name I often used in the nineties. It was published as an Above Ground chapbook in 1998, and reprinted in 2004, after the publisher found out who Ms. Field was.

"Imaginary Poems for AMB" were addressed to my late wife Angela in the months that followed her death.

"He Is Not!" is of course a micro-translation of Shelley's "Adonais." It is a companion piece to my poem "Do Sink," which was just the opposite—an expansion of a Keats sonnet.

Many of the poems in this book were germinated in secret ways. The one for the Gzowski golf tournament is obvious. "Victor's Secret" is less so—Victor is a dog who channelled several poets, including P. K. Page and Rachel Wyatt, and produced *Victor's Verses*, published by Outlaw Editions.

There are eight tributes to other writers, in a series that has been running in several of my books. These are sentence-poems commissioned for obits or *Festschrifts*, and there must be thirty of them by now.

"Lost in the Library" was first commissioned by the CBC, then made into a Backwoods Broadside (Maine), and then recreated as a music video with the Duncan Hopkins jazz trio, directed by Elvis Prusic for Blink Pictures and Bravo!FACT.

That other apparent series made of the word "She" followed by a verb in the ongoing present? I hope that it just keeps on going. "She" is my sweetheart, Ms. Baird, and action words refer to her very well, thank you.

The last sequence in this book has had a history. A narrative essay called "How I Wrote One of My Poems" told the story of "Grandfather" and how that anthology piece was written. The essay was published in my memoir *A Magpie Life* (Key Porter, 2001). By the time I came to delivering a lecture at Capilano College, at the invitation of Jenny Penberthy, my attempts to assassinate that poem had resulted in a longer essay and some strange rewriting of the grandfilial exercise.

Then in 2005, after I had composed eight versions of the benighted poem, Meredith and Peter Quartermain published the result as a nice chapbook for their Nomados press. That version turned out to be the longest one, with material that added fictional biography to something purporting to be an essay, just as here the essay, with a little less fictional biography, brings a book of poetry to rest.

And you know what they say the rest is.

Composition

                          is composure's lack,
uneasy setting of items
side by side,
                a shining fish
on a counter

counts, one counts and two
puts an end to it
for now.

        Then
there's another now, and its track
is for keeping,
                and this
one, two,
            is how we do it,
we three.

Sitting in Vancouver

Sitting in Vancouver: Children's Hospital Caf

Woman with cheap brown hair
& two kids,
delightful daughter, legs
folded beneath her,
bright-eyed over Jell-O

& brother, head bent in isolation,
no book, a video game? is he lorn
or is he bud of painful lovely
future, dreaming alone,
being, perhaps,
me?

Chinese woman stares
at setting sun, black cedar tips,
her hands wrapt around tea.

—Where does she
truly live?   Where is her life?

Where are their lives hidden?
Written—

Where is mine,
gone?

My dear woman in a machine
reading hers, another chapter,

a good sentence or two?

Sitting in Vancouver: Gynecology Clinic, Broadway

Women's names uttered quietly

    inane folksong radio

            they
are pregnant or grey

        gone
from time to time to back rooms,

       what
is there besides *thousands* of files
  in sliding shelves

    A black hat
  a good man
    sitting side
      by side

In this women's place
    where woman's name
  "Doctor"
      is spoken on the phone

not necessarily beauty
    at the door.

Sitting in Vancouver: Central Station

Can I get a one-way
            to Squ'awsh, he says,
bus riders, words
            all over their clothes.

who the hell works here?
                        offers hard-eye love
            at most

not a ghost in this place,
no real
            tracks, no smell of sausage

this train station's
                        a museum, like
the notion of Calgary

Old people with vague
            north Europe accent
going to Kaslo, only reality
            I've seen. So there is,

but there isn't
                        a train with
            my sister on it

Sitting in Vancouver: Multiple Sclerosis Clinic

Dada brains
   young, mostly, poorly
dressed
  or upcountry,
     limp beside husbands, charts
  mysterious on walls,
      plastic
spine bones
  a *motif,* you might say.

   They think about lunch
   and parking meters

—bacteria float in the air
  like words, like a simile
 looking for a place to land,
like iambic gnats.

  Behind doors cheerful doctors
keep up their spirits.
    Haven't seen
  a politician for hours,
   haven't read anything
   better than Gautier
   for years.

Sitting in Vancouver: SFU Cafeteria

Can't believe all the fat boys,
      fat girls
             lined up for burgers
fries and Coke.

            Tomorrowland
rocket off the lapel

                 yeah, yeah
she says,

            Burroughs wouldn't be here
grumbling with necktie,

Allen wouldn't be here, Atwood,
she wouldn't be here

                no fancy
basketball shoes, what's that?
a slurpee!
          jumbo, two straws—

primary idiots keep these chairs
from lifting away,
              get the hang of it

yeah, that's good, she says.

Sitting in Vancouver: Vancouver Hospital Laurel Pavilion

Fat women pushing walkers,
         walking wounded,
                  whoosh of air door—

One forgets inside
                  —it's grey and
looks but isn't, soft.

         They are, but their
week is hard, hard to look at—
         airplanes can fall on roofs,
                           who cares?

   I'll be back, she says,
         did you find that chart,
she says—female voices
                  still here,   young
in uniform,   still don't know
   their lives are stories.

         I know them, know
how they come out.   Even these
   smooth thin ones,
               names on their chests.

Sitting in Vancouver: Student Pub

Noise at big windows.
    peculiar music pounding
            out of something black,
more black than this beer—

        Where are the poets,
are they over in Toronto, under
    the curvature, wet leaves clumped
in front of red brick cubes, poets

    drinking coffee and newspapers.

    Here homely girls shoot pool.
        I could suicide easily.

In Küsnacht it drew dark early,

    here the carpet is the colour
    of Martian innards.

    If I were a pen
        I would be a girl pen

beautiful as a grey boat in the lake,
    under water,
                insensible
not writing but sitting,

            having forgotten language
unable to grasp a chicken
    in my sister's yard.

Hate chicken meat, grey on legs,
            love the word.

Sitting in Vancouver: UBC Hospital

In Emergency
      they're all old
           & no hair combed,

got blue shiny shins,
      harrup, up on bed,
      who knows last time
      they ever read

like anything, a book?
      Is this a waste of life,
is this a drum with no fife?

Is this a revolution
      in the wrong country,

do they look at you
      askance or not
         at all?

Were any of them ever tall?

Sitting in Winnipeg: West End Cultural Centre

Cold Indians on Balmoral,
    skiff o' Hallowe'en snow—

I've been like a goose
    went north, why's that?

        —music in foreign language
or some speaker inside

          wends black like me.

Who could walk to that beat?

      my old short time
Métis girlfriend,
        I made her arm green

wearing my ID bracelet in Manitoba.

Was that history
or mistake—
        did I play

electric guitar a week ago
          in Port
   Colborne?

      Am I dying,
meester?

Sitting in Vancouver: Vancouver International Airport

Prince George passengers
            watching space opera on TV

What's it called?
            Used to see it in hospital—

Here healthy teens with backpacks
            hitchhike jet planes

            —hideous carpet
would hide puke easy,
            planning we pay for, bud.

Snap coka can, stretch leg,
            mumble in Alien,

I been there, but I never learned
            how to do that with my gum, lady.

You gotta live there,
            Prince George, I mean,

where I'll look around ironic,
            sleep like a lizard
            on the plane
            back.

Words on Water?

What lorn poet prays to gods long gone
from ocean's glistening wrack, what beach
on edge of that deep book can offer comfort
never found by parlour fire? If read he must
why reads he not indoors, from tomes endited
centuries afore, beaker full of the warm
South close to hand? But no, this wind-swept
gent ambles in the rain, shoes wet with punc-
tuation from the sea, fishing for words
in language known but to spectres lost to
memory. Send him welcome, dry yourself,
invite, come finger our shelves so proudly
stacked with words on paper. Here will gulls
keen and sea-creatures play while reader
warms his haunch beside the grate. Here
will flames read to us their living tongue,
and speak the words that viewless wings have sung.

While

It took a while
to get here
and when I got here
I had grown older.

A, You're Adorable

by Ellen Field

An alphabet book for Wilbur Snowshoe

A

(now do I really want an indefinite
Article?)

is for Apple, a pull, an Article
the original Adam could have done
without.

A dam did it to him, they say,
damned him, poor man
silly horse,
to definite
deth.

O riginal letter, looks forward & up
At the same time, that pull, is the Be
ginning of time.
I did not even want
to talk About it. I did not
start All this.

I would have given him
a peach, started the sentence
with a push,
started with a P,
definite-
ly.

39

B

(not really Beginning But

gun, or as he would say
on the way
to a Big inning, just past
one.

Can we lose a past,

gun it down

if it persists,

isters?

What do we have to have
in our Bonnets? No questy
one, I am not Eve.
not Steve, either/or Adam
ant e'en about
tit.

These are not apples
nor are we out & about
to get Back in
a knee time soon.

No acts, no judges,
no time for kings
when the mask era
smudges.

C

}
BC

PR

NR

AF

& all the brave men
who built them, a his
tory of my Country, told initially
straight-faced.

       Stray facts,
like the neighbours? Oh say
Can (you see) a day
go by, some dollars go buy
south.

Women who were not even there
watched them go by. Not
from sea to sea, but shining
like top soil in the wind.

C (BS)
Coming back north
Weighed down with anchor-men.

D

} feet went over

fence before

tail

but I have always
lived for the last.

(shoemaker)
De-ranged, fenced in,
lasting for the leaves, longing,
leaving at last, Dropping
really over the thing,
almost Defenceless, nearly
footloose, loving every De-
tail since.

Make a sentence,
he said, containing. I knew
I had to hightail it,
Design a life
where the grass is in
Deed greener.

E

nough, that's my in
itial, I can't get out of it
more than I put in.
      Initial

E I was some
one Else, was it Else
E,
was it any
one, an E one could trust?

Does one Equal m
see squared, I mean, or E means,
really squared, Even
if you (you) don't know what
that means? Is it all
the same?

   Enuff of questions,
how about if 'E gives us (you and me)
nothing but answers from now
on
  paper, or something.

F

you too, I told him, imagine:
men speak to their women
that way now. You two, I said,

you and your woe, man.
What an image, a man
using the F word in speech
with his ex-woman, she
on the spot, he
marking it.
His sign.
           I did like to F
with him, though, and now
woe is me,
I will probableed
have to start all
over again,

oh men.

G

spot, he called it,

I'm looking for your G spot, he said.

Golly, I said, are you a
spot man, or a letterman, maybe
a G-man?

Pretty
spotty wooing, I calls it, and he
quit looking. Now he's found
something else.

I thought,
he said, you Girls wanted us Guys
to look for it.

No, I replied, we
would like you
to look for us look,

we leopards, we have Spots, pard,
like you never dreamed of, you
might try to make us change them.

H

is the favourite letter
of my favourite poet. Hello there,

and Help me, will you, nobody
knows my name, and they all
know your initials.

Would you write me a letter
of introduction. Dear fave,
help me now and in the Hour
of my greatest reading. You
Have the Hours, a book
few people read and fewer
write.

Soon,

      Mother
or an   other
organ

.

I

went with me and myself
to a party, and boy
were we lonesome.

I
dentify yourself, said a toothy soul
and no One else
spoke to us all night.

No propositions for the prepositions.
You should have been there
but he wasn't. Could have said
care to dance? Got ance
in your pance?

Got not
anyone in my sight
all night. All right, I
shouldn't have been there,
no place for me and myself.

Only old tooth and his truth,
evil I.

J

birds, he said, we were as
naked as J birds, delighted

we were not wearing so much
as a J cloth (pat. reg.).
                    Gets much cooler
  and we'll be blue Jays, I said.
                    (I crowed)

But it was fun, it was sun
in September, remember, no one

goes skinny dipping in September,
especially if skinny.

              Nak*ed*
he said, de-
lighted.

We're past
participals, I said, pass me
an artical of clothing, but

Just one more minute, he said.
It's late summer and we

are in it. I, ally, Jumped
once more, in.

K,

I said, you just struck out
swinging.

Strike three, I shouted,
right hand raised high.

Lucky for me he wasn't a hitter,
and I wasn't out to be struck,

what luck. He was nothing
and three, nothing raised high,

no longer even hope. You can
Kiss off but not me, I cried

in the bottom of the ninth.
Kisses on the bottom, he managed,

you ain't gottem. He wasn't
much of a swinger, even.

You're out, I added, sorry
about your average.

So are you, he said,
first time he got wood on it all year.

L

fa
bet

a better elf than poet's debt,
a muse
meant to divert
the two green sides of any
one's brain.

So Law
tea
dough done just right,
an afternoon deLight
that's Legal.

Oh L
said, Ellen,
well fed, perfectly in-spired

imperfectly out-
erred
      but out there utterly
and heavier
than the atmos
fair

A Letter from my Love.

M

end
as you go
along

that's My advice.
Start with that in Mind
and don't be afraid to change it.

The or
M, be ready to depart
from your be
ginning, re M
bering it is all
Middle.

Where else, you
pecker head?

M
brace it all, the end
is nigh,
in the be
ginning is My
Middle.

N

o, I said
because he seemed particularly
dense, and then
because he seemed particularly
insensitive to his density,
that spells No, I explained.

Yes, I did. Not a particle
of sense seemed to enter that head,
a ten-watt bulb in there.

O, I said
because he was looking for yes,
No you don't.

I was growing
tense, there was a spell
there when I didn't know
whether he would take No
even if I told him the letters
waiting for an answer.

I swear it was intense
until he gave up generally
on the question.

Buckley Bay

O

round, O
world, where On your sure face
will I find the bend
          that bends for me?

The be all and end all;
the ball bounces more than Once,
and I bounce On it, wondering

where O where
will the circle become square,
the bend all flat,
where I'll know, O where I'm at?

I'm bound,
On my way
but all tied up.

I've never found,
never have I found dead
what was Only started,

nor found a live
ending, a live O.

I've wanted to be low
where the sure face
would never be turned
to ward me
Off.

P

you, I told him,
you give off a P
culiar let us say
redolence.

        He read
my meaning, co-
rectly, having had a bath
an hour ago,
he knew I meant the violence
of his oh
Pinion.

        You can't Pin me
down, I have to fly, I said,
red in the face, I ex-
Pect, from my efforts,
oral as they only were.

Q

        -tip, I called you
because of your soft white head.

A soft man
is hard to find.

Q-tip, o,
Q, you I teased, you softly
stayed at your ease,

your eyes hardly open,
softly closed.
             Your moving blood.

I miss you, Q,
your lip, your
tibia in my grip,

your grey turned white,
your girth, your height,
my legs that could nearly
manage both, especially

your Quiet

in the face of my riot.

I need you for my diet,
you old
stick in the mud.

R

and R, performing seal,
I think that and that's all I was
for you—

Are you happier now
than I? Happier than the Rest

or the Rest I brought you, the Re-
creation? We made it, that's all
you thought, I think.

Therefore I am
making this happy
ur-poem of your quick Re-
treat. More happy, happy still un-
Ravished groom, at Rest

I'm making Room

to flush you out,
to seal your doom.

S

nake, yeah
S
you are.

S.u.r.
e.
lated to See
me naked
and a
frayed nerve outside a body.

A Sheer
dance in air, above,
in the buff, your
hiss,
      your twist,
                yess,
your mind there
on the ground.

T

D, you called it, a
Three-point play, you said,
a bases-loaded, I Think
you said, home run. You
called it a one-Two punch.

It felt more like
a short-
handed goal
from a scramble
in front.

U

biquitous, that's what you are.
Everywhere I look out for myself
there you are
           looking in.

God's, maybe I should imagine,
gift to women,
you are omni
           present.

           You bitch, that's what you
whisper to me every time,
always looking out for yourself.
Won't give some-one-else
a look in.

           Unwrap it your-
self, that's my advice,
there's a virtue in being
nowhere
at once.

V

for Vic Tory you thought,
laying on the liberal
Varnish,
    till I be
came here today gone to
morrow.

    Your shining's
tar. Politics and star-making
never were your long
suits.
    (How I hated your clothes.)

    Just this side
of celestial bodies
I was Vanished, like a V
of wild geese, and you,

you were just the north.

see, I said When
he said Where
you going?

To We
We, I said, to get a
Way from us.

I had to go
Where a Woman
has to go.

To point Polly
at the porcelain
as they say in Western
Australia.

Are you coming back,
he Wanted to know.

I only said
I got to go.

And I Went
as they say
West.

X

might mark the spot
but I am not the spot,

not your dog, sir,
not ready to wag your tail.

Call me your unknown quantity,
call me the cross you have to bear;

(call but don't whistle)

you can mark and you can bark
but I'm not voting in the dark.

There was a time
you thought you'd spotted a mark.

That ugly line
is all yours, you plug
without a spark.

Y

knot, You kept saying, trying
to tie me down. Why not

let me tie You up, You said,
it's a bond.

     It's a bind, I kept
replying, Yes braiding again,
I want no strings attached,
not even Your favourite
note in Gee.

     Aw, letter
down, Your hair, You whined,
and let me dine at the Y.

Not I, no when, no what,
no why.

     No way. Now I
unbraid a way from You
every day. A fork in every road,

and this miss leaves You
the road untaken.

Z

you,
something or other—

I'm so sleepy

after all this, what
is your voice—

Zo sleepy, I
have to get

what's that?

Zleep—

Three Political Falltime Haiku

Yellow maple leaf

falls from branch nearest the clouds

glides off gun barrel

Ripples on Meech Lake

die before reaching a shore

Mulroney phones Bush

N D P O K

It's fall in Ontario?

Not at all—it's spring.

Fragment, Trieste, December 1981

je reviendrai le long du Grand Canal
regarder les embarcations, le dôme bleu
de San Antonio Taumaturgo …
    —Nicole Brossard

6:15 p.m. Friday, train station filled
with Yugoslavians sitting, men and women
squatting on the floor, each surrounded
by lettered plastic shopping sacks
filled with "Western" goodies. The body
is a bad neighbourhood.

They fill mineral water bottles
from the men's room tap.
Women with huge earrings, bright
not new scarves and skirts, are
clearly themselves.

The younger men look poor,
not Triestinos in their old
black shoes and pants, a few drunk with
girlfriends, try for Italian cock-
iness. No slav nation.

2. (No subtle subtitle)

In the rain every Triestino has a good
umbrella. Cars parked up the sidewalk,
traffic of Renaults and Fiats, little guys
under the karsk, jammed on Corso Italia,
moving a baroque block in ten minutes.

I went to look again at the Roman theatre
in lonely dark, saw once again a portentous
calm power. The ludic is lucid.

Every store on the Corso is selling clothes
and shoes and handbags, Italians everywhere
romantic with leather, here the fashion
not *outré* as Milan, but proud. Ah Vienna, ah
Rome. Imbalanced, ambu-
latory, still, you have to see your body
from where your head is.

3.

We don't see Triestinos agreeing with the usual
wisdom that their city's a sad sentimental
declassé survivor of its own importance.

The cab driver has stereo speakers,
No Smoking sign and pack of Marlboroughs
on the dash. Heavy baroque Viennese walls
with Italian chain-store neon slide by. People
on sidewalks wait for the *Avanti* sign,
and if they don't the driver gives them
an even break.

We watched television in the Albergo Corso
lobby, a film about early revolutionary China.
It's not a great restaurant city, given to bars
and taverns and *trattorias*. There's no Xmas
overkill, only very discreet offerings,
boxed sets of brandy and champagne in the bar,
a Santa Claus on the side of our hotel, one block
of scant coloured lights overhead. No salvation.

4.

I listened to nineteen fifties jazz on my FM radio,
Shorty Rogers, etc. The new jazz guys come to
play in Padua, but not Trieste, listen to the
silent strains of Strauss. But at the train station
there are more happy family welcomes than in
any other city in North Italy.

These narrow streets accept rain as their
milieu. No matter thick clogged traffic,
I hear few hits on high-pitched Fiat horn.
Oops, now there's Booker Erwin on the jazz
station. He co-insides.

The Yugoslavians bringing their folded
money to Trieste to buy jeans and cigarettes
like Canadians windowshopping in Seattle and
Detroit. No slave nation.

5.

We drink a nice house merlot and tocai at the
Trieste Mia *trattoria,* where dessert is decidedly
Vienna, pastries, mousses, cakes with chocolate
architecture. We indulge a taste for German and Danish
beer. Braided bread is a tapastry.

God, one comes back to Trieste, back
to the same hotel. There are pockets of French
cigarette smoke in the air over sidewalks and tables.
Under red roofs of Austria's own Mediterranean.
Swiss radio on as I scribble, peculiar German,
and I turn the shortwave knob—Russian, Albanian,
BBC, US empire.

6.

Thea found twelve black and white cats
among a pack of pigeons being, it may be,
tended by an old woman, loose black sweater,
behind the Roman Theatre. Quick
build-up of roiling dark clouds off the Adriatic,
fetched against the karsk.

                    All over town
young men with jacks changing tires on Fiats
with Croatian license plates.

The seven-story Hapsburg walls, yellow from
the fourth floor up, big shutters, heavy stone
face with lateral stripes, high carved doors,
Neptune and fishes, pillared windows on top story.
statues on the edge of roof. Stephen
Daddyless was born on the seventh floor.

7.

After all this descriptive setting it is interesting
to be standing on the parapet of St. Giusto castle
while the first bora of the year blows down
off the Belgrade flats over the karsk, so one is nearly
lifted over the hill and city into the sea, very blue
this December 19, beyond the red roofs of Trieste.
I saw a drama on Io, a diorama.

The ridge of dark green mountains with that odd
immense memorial so threatening and pitiless
on that high horizon, not here yet, but near. I
prefer uninteresting clothes hanging in tented stalls
at Ponterossa market for weekend Slavs, a
contra-pun tale, Nora.

8.

Il Piccolo newspaper, founded 1881, centennial
headline shows little change, desperate strike by
Solidarity in Polish crisis—photo of Polish tourists
sleeping in their car in Trieste—come to buy
blue jeans, don't want to motor back to Gdansk
during military takeover.

                I bought two
folding umbrellas. They keep blowing
inside out in the wind that is cut into instant
changes of direction by angular streets
of Trieste. The guy that sold me the umbrellas
looked at my credit card and saw that I
am from Canada. He asked whether I speak
French. I said there is not much French
on the Pacific coast. "Van*couv*er," he said. Yes.
"Saskatchewan is in the middle," he said. Yes.
Poetic prose, he said, cess.

9.

Youngsters are bellowing all day Saturday through
megaphones, handing out pamphlets about helping
the efforts of the Polack pope and Lech Walesa.

We climbed the Giant's Stairway
and came down through memorial park,
seeing that one family lost a man in World War One
and three men in World War Two. We found
Stephen Deadlist, then we toured
the Old City, and came out in the Piazza of
United Italy, and for the first time I saw an
Italian fountain with icicles hanging from it.

Yet in the morning, walking the beach at Miramare,
we'd seen a man, grey and balding, swimming
in the Adriatic. He climbed out over big square rocks,
and he was in good trim, wearing only swim briefs,
here, in the Penthouse of the Western World.

10.

In the lunch café we were introduced to baby
Amanda, ugly little thing who had just been,
aged two months, christened today, Amanda
in her fancy white dress, her big family
having an immense long meal at Fabris.

Christmas trees are just now making their
appearance, December 20. Swiss
radio station plays jazz all day, and it is
cool to hear Sonny Rollins instead of white
Christmas in the morning.

                    Italo Svevo
Bookshop publishes lots of books about
the region of Trieste. Whether it is a function
or denial of the usual wisdom *re* Trieste's
decline and inferiority feelings, Triestinos
seem quite happy to be both Italian
(as shown in the art of eating, which they perform
perfectly yet without pretension) and not
the rest of Italy. You will find
perfect *krauti* as one of your vegetables
at dinner, your trout will remind you of Austria's
best.

11.

Trieste's shiny little automobiles
do not have dents in the fenders,
clocks on buildings keep the right time
and chime when they should.

                We stood
in the gorgeous Serbian Orthodox church
next to the Ponterossa, filled as it is with
white candles the size of upright logs, and
listened to the mass, and there was only
a handful of worshippers, more properly
attendees, there.

12.

Watching evening news, Poland, the pope, soccer
etc., we saw the Italian TV news readers
move their hands expressively while reading
the news, maybe a little less than Italians might do
in the streets. They want a relationship
with invisible us. The news
wants to be history, poetry
is a stowaway on history.

The incestuous ancestors of our
Triestinos speak to us
in waves against a cold continent,
a language we do not know.

First Thing

First thing I did today,
read a Charles Bernstein poem
while drinking guava juice, didn't
even think of going
                          back to bed.
                          Phone keeps ringing
anyway, kind of like
          in a Bernstein poem.
I'm waiting to do a Platonic
crossword puzzle, but my neck hurts
from tension!   everyone in the house
hates me this morning. I bring them
everything but poetry.

An Old Manuscript about Breasts

When women lie on their backs
their breasts slip to the side and nearly disappear.

When they lean forward on ten-speed bikes
their breasts hang like oriole nests.

Schoolgirls hug their largest textbooks
vertical against their breasts.

When bank tellers reach down for blank cheques
they show their breasts have light freckles.

I poked my nose into my mother's
nineteen-year-old breasts* when I was two days old.
I can't remember what they looked like.
I can't remember seeing them at all.

---

* Well, she was nineteen. One could argue about the age of her breasts, I suppose.

ASQ

a squid,
a liquid
with arms
it squirms through dark,
a lisquirm
in the deep,
arms reaching for light.

It is like nothing,
lithe as no thing.
It is like you.

Imaginary Poems for AMB

I do this all the time,
and this
writing in your notebook,

I learn that John Zarelli
wrote a history of Oliver
        before he died
and I say I will
        show it to you—

such simple words, a rush
of real forgetting
because you may have
        known him, or
his daughter, old now

in the local paper, how
I look at the familiar sun
on the apple blossoms—

think how we desired
        to be here in April—

our daughter's eyes, blossoms,
sun on blue mountain's grace.

She saw it this morning,

I am surrounded by
        your female in-laws,

I could die here,
        there'd be few to notice.

I saw the garden
        where you watched
                me dance with my mother.

We knew then
        it was a momentous day.

Here's another. We are
        almost here.

I wonder if you send me
    my dreams of you—

Did I do something that day
    to deserve your visit—

When we made love last night
    was it for my last reading—

If I intend good thoughts
    will I be too full of myself—

If I write poems for your ear
    am I talking to myself—

Is it when mind is empty
    and needful you come,
    a gift you were ready to give,
    a forgiveness I have held
    from myself—

Miss Silver Heels
in Dublin

where you didn't
bother keeping
up. You knew

more than I know
even now.

Even now I look
at the dark between
dark green leaves

and there
you are, silver

picked by handicapped
sun. You were my

only book of kells.

The special
hardly ever
wine you
bought me

we six drank
last night after
a '62 poem
for you, reverently

spoken by our
daughter as I
was tongue-tied
then untied

by your gift, all
thirty-seven
years, how curious
they were, and
it was.

When I get to Heaven
can I stay with you
till one of your younger men
arrives?

Will you see me
from time to time
in Eternity?

Will there be something
I can do for you?

Will you believe me again
when I say I love you
still more?

I am surrounded by ghosts
here in this ghost world.

They are all alive
they say, you are looking good
they say.

I don't tell them
I only want to be where
I can look at you, even
from a distance
if there is distance there

and that is not
what I want here.

Why in my dreams
do you seem so
hopeful, or careless
of hope?

          Even when I know
what I know you are
here, no synonym, a
comfortable present, a

drop against despair. You
visit and I know
no rest on waking,
my hand over

your diminishing hip
knows, it can even
tell me, you
are there, but

what is there?

You squint your eyes
in girl's delight
& sniff the baby's head

or so I see you
from our bed, iamb
following iamb, image

maintained, like a suite
inspected by a mother.
The baby is

driving my car across town;
this is the century
we all wanted you to

see, those eyes wide
& still green after all
these tears.

I'm Still

First time
in ten years

I look into
the first mirror

in the Fort Saint
John airport john.

Good! I'm still
in there,

Islands

This time of year I dream of islands, the smell of sea, smell of the pendulous flowers. I long to swim out in the warm turquoise waters of their safe lagoons. I dream of clearly delineated constellations turning in the night sky, and of a full moon rising suddenly out of the sea, bathing everything with its strange lunar light. It makes me thankful for my life, blessed to be witness to a universe that is truly benign. This time of year my nose longs for the smell of frangipani, my tongue for the taste of coconut.

Dear Ken,
I've been there.
I know the scent.
But today in the Kerrisdale gym
I was riding the bike for the first time in a month.
The smell was my sweat, the oldness of the machine,
a drift of liniment from another room.
I was reading your book, and while this page was open
tropical flowers crept upon me.
As far as I know, this is no metaphor,
the scent I remember with an ache surrounded me.
It was mid-afternoon, late summer, Wednesday,
what was there to long for?

Sometimes I

Sometimes I look at the world
and sometimes I pass it through my body.

Sometimes I have paint on my hands
and sometimes my stomach oozes.

These conditions led me in my youth
to look for a woman I could mistake for poetry.

Whether I succeeded is left for loving critics to decide
while I pick at the steep sides of this hole.

The world seems not to notice my intent
as I pass through it, quarter by quarter.

It is the earth, not the world, you dolt,
she told me while I only gaped through lidded eyes.

Years after I began this nonsense I returned
only proving that I'd grown stupid over the years.

Six Little Poems in Alphabetical Order

A Child of Nine

9 9

Metro Spring

The apparition
of these white chickens

in the crowd, petals
on a wet red wheelbarrow

Pictures from Bill

According to Williams
when Icarus fell
it was no big deal.

There Is

There is a creek.

And there is an underground creek
that can be located in old maps.

And there is a human body
such as that worn by Heraclitus

that can measure the creek
by walking beside it.

This poem was found by Roger Farr, in an e-mail message I sent to a group called
easter-island@sfu.ca.

Thin 41st Ave. Poem Written on a Bookmark

Middle-aged
beautiful woman
weighed down arms
with two plastic
grocery sacks.

I like her more
than the thin
mother trying to
look sexy
as her daughter.

Unknown Liquid

Every morning I drop
      a little unknown liquid
onto my right eye.

That moment it sees
      the shiny bead arriving
is the prettiest sight all day.

He Is Not!: A Quick Elegy

Oh Damn, he died and I know when.
His muse was squatting like a hen.

Oh Lady, just go back to sleep,
Or for the blind old guy, do weep.

A lot of poets come and go.
This last one was your finest, though.

He had to go and die in Rome,
And lie there in his final home.

Now all his waking dreams there sag,
And spill their tears on every rag.

They break their bows and cut their hair,
And one just kissed him lying there.

Yet others come, his spirits made,
And all of nature seems afraid.

No longer will his echo sound.
The flowers fall onto the ground.

His eagle screams up in the sky.
The spring has come to taunt my eye.

All nature seems to croon with life,
Except our moment's sharpest knife.

Yes, life goes on, and follows grim,
For waking will not come to him.

A storm released
came from the east.

But here's the muse, on tender feet.
The face of Death is like a beet.

Unto the poet she says "Speak,
"You never should have died this week.

"B. chased the critics all away,
"And left their corpses where they lay."

Then came the poets, M. and B.,
And one more wraith, who looked like me.

He seemed a lamp just going out,
An injured creature faint with doubt.

The others saw his wounded brow,
And heard this phantom whisper now:

Who left you poison in your cup?
Unlovely shit-bespattered pup!

He'll turn to ash, but here is fire
Gone from us, but soaring higher.

Like figures on an ancient urn,
He's out of time in its quick turn.

His voice is everywhere to hear.
It makes a muddled nature clear.

Now love and life join in his climb
To poets dead before their time.

The singing in that kingless sphere
Should rouse our lesser music here.

The fame of all our Romes will fade,
But in their ruins grows a glade:

There lies a body ever new,
And there is earth awaiting you.

Do linger there if you would rise;
This pretty world is all that dies.

A light shines on me in this dark,
And welcomes my communal spark.

There's the back
of a slender neck
    just below slightly
curled hair, tilted
    just so—

Why can't I simply
    enjoy my death,
how can this go on,
    this, given
lovely irritation. I

    have got this far
with nothing, will proceed
    with nothing, but
some pernicious god
    sets only a little

beyond your hand's reach
    what your fingers
would so naturally
    want to deliver
news to.

Egg

The first time she saw me crack a hard-boiled egg
on my forehead—did I vex her or delight her? For
me vexation and delight are synonymous. As long
as I am doing it.

An Arm Whose Purpose

An arm whose purpose
is reach for the keys

no help to her, out of home
over montañas to this eight

never gathered before, hello
Lou, you're north again

can't stay out of love
don't see down the table—

is this eating or is this
travel or is this

shit, who knows? Can you
write to order

some dessert, the keys white
under black fingers

illuminate somebody's soul anyway
a luminous numinous

never filled this lad's stomach, never
got past the first round.

"Shortly After Takeoff"

"shortly after takeoff"
fantasy never did anyone

no good, elbows out
at the elbows, hope

in the wrong airport, love
none of your business—

can you make it for seven
o'clock, are the young

too angry for conversation, is
your mind any place for privacy?

Can I come over and lay my concerns
on your former self, did you

know I was coming? That room,
Señora, it means

nothing to me now, nothing
is my fervent wish.

A Brief Poem in the Kroetsch Manner

My mother said don't touch that pie.

My mother left the room.

I touched the pie.

The PGI Golf Tourney Poetic Address and Apology for Same

Since T. S. Eliot
every modern poem begins
with a quotation from the classics, say
Shakespeare's *As You Like It*:

All the world's a golf course,
And all the men and women merely duffers.
They have their tee shots and their swear words,
And one chump in his time plays many holes.
At first the infant
Mewling and puking in the nurse's arms,
Till the nurse sees her husband and lets go.
Then the whining school boy with his golf bag.
Creeping like a snail toward the bunker on four.
Then a shanker, full of strange oaths, and bearded like a goat,
Seeking a lost ball in the rough.
Where the nurse quickly stands up and adjusts her uniform.
Then the justice, in fair round belly with good single malt lined,
Eyes severe and nose quite ruddy, making a pitch shot
By hand when no one's looking.
Last scene of all, that ends this strange eventful tourney,
Is second childishness, another seven-stroke green,
And weeping in the arms of the nurse,
Sans teeth, sans eyes, sans trousers, sans everything.

Thus William Shakespeare, to later and lesser poets
known as the Leader Bard.

Let me introduce myself, a lesser poet
sponsored for this occasion by Petro-Canada;
call me Dick Assboy, get me on Letterman.

Make me literate, man; I've read bill bissett's
poem of last year, and didn't understand
one word! Help me read
the *Literacy B.C.* newsletter, man; quote:
"*higher* profile for ... *foundational* skills."

What do I know
about golfing for literacy? Can I read a lie?
(Did I ever *hear* a lie on a golf course?)
My brother plays eighteen holes every day,
but he can't read bill bissett's poetry.

I think that golfers speak their own poetry.
I heard Vicki Gabeareau intone:
"Drive for show—putt for beer!"

Or look to the Bible, from whence cometh
our pro: "Ask, and it shall be given thee;
seek, and thou shalt find; putt,
and it shall be opened unto thee."
                              —Matthew VII, 7

2.

Let me introduce Muriel Honey,
driver of my golf cart,
three-wood of my heart.
Muriel Honey doesn't slow for corners,
understands what's supposed to be in the cup.
Gzowski never warned me
my driver gathers all beer tickets from tee-
totallers; she had one at every tee,
what a total!

3.

I am a recovering golfer, I took
the eighteen-step program.
My brother is always on the green in two;
I'm on the couch by three. Numbers
mean everything to him and me.

I'm no Dave Barr; call me Sand Bar.
That's the trap I fall into,
where my caddy sneaks up behind me
and gives me a wedgie.

I'm too erratic for this game.
The regular golfer
goes to the John Daily.

It gets worse: Dick Zokol's brother Ron
is my dental surgeon; unlike his brother,
he always makes the cut.

4.

It could be worse.
This could be verse.
I could make cut
a rime for putt.

But I won't.

I'll end this nonsense at the nineteenth hole
with thank-yous for the rigmarole,
to Peter Mansbridge and all of yous,
who prove that readers *are* the news.

Victor's Secret

The odours! Not the sea
but the septic field beside the sea.

I run iambic over smells
enamour me of humans,

persuade me to frisk, lift nose,
inhale Mike, dream of sausage.

What a doggish place is this
I visit now as opposite

to punishing. I swim
when they are not watching.

I cavort with arfing seals
and dry myself enhidden.

I sleep upon their bed
and never leave a wrinkle,

not a winkle, nary a wink,
no reminder when I pee into the sink!

How Odd Men Are, Really

Women
take off their rings
and leave them on shelves,
tabletops.

Their legs below dark coats
cross intersections
in the rain.

And we wait in automobiles
for news from distant quarters.

Ryan Finds

Ryan finds
his skin
important—

eyes, or one
eye looks at you
under curious
brow—

touch him, lead
him through
darkness to
the chair—

eye only completes
his face,
feet keep him there.

The Important Stuff on Granville Island

Even when there's no parking on Granville Island
there's poetry.

Even when there's no island at Granville Island
there's Granville Island Lager.

& poets like lager, prose writers too,
they like lager.

Even when there's no beer-drinking poets on Granville Island
there's poetry, or if we're lucky, fudge.

I have a friend who sells fudge on Granville Island,
mmm, boy.

Even when there's no poetry on Granville Island
there's fudge.

Unlikely Childhood Transculturation

I was always
reading de Maupassant
to Obasan.

She was
an Okinawan
from the Okanagan.

Long Melted

Iceland Arnason, isn't that nice to say? Iceland Arnason the Gimli
girth, a Scanadian to like.

He and Birk Sproxton sat together in Calgary, leaning away from
the speaker, Angela called them the Big Boys.

Noise, don't you love the way he talks Canadian prairie, voice that
says Cooooley, and you know there's a bearded chuckle coming.

Never, despite all that theory, forgot how to tell stories, saga man,
ice long melted from his whiskers.

I see new painted white rail fences, long green pastures, some lost
country north of Wetaskiwin, no that's Neepawa, very neat, not a
straggle.

Except this guy's laughter, not unlike a sneeze, old Snori would
have told, a story broached or Kroetsched, a singular man, our
Dave.

I always want to pat his belly, like there's a baby in there, soon to
be born, it's Dave himself the natal story, Island Arnason.

You can't get away from it, Manitoba Dave, out in the breathing
cloud, determined to get this car going, laughing when we should
be freezing.

No fooling, there's a long poem in that Winnipeg bar, and Dave
is just coming in the door, he is ready to eat.

Coils

The number of times we needed something and there she was with something I can't tell you.

She used to iron her famous hair before it was all that famous, this was in Toronto where the rivers are gone.

Hardly anyone knows about the famous pajamas so I am not about to break the news here but they were sometimes red.

She always knows someone who can do just the thing you need so badly that if life were to go on without her, how could it.

Peggy, she's not exactly leggy, but she can move faster than you can, even when she seems to be sitting still, in a rocking chair, with a caftan, and a kitten.

Can you think of anything she hasn't written, neither can I, and I have been around longer than you have, and it seems as if she just got here.

Someone said you can't put a comma after a first person singular, does that have anything to do with anything?

She said that in French her name will be du Bois, but no one I know ever thought of calling her Whitey.

If there is a heaven, I'm hoping to see her there, but with my luck she'll be sitting at the gate with a fountain pen and a big book.

Ah, the world of literature pokes its nose in everywhere, preventing some people from being the immortal home economics teachers they could have been.

Poet, that's easier to say. Novelist. Voice on the phone. Really good friend.

Her Moment, Ours

She's lived a poem and composed a life, and for once, for once, one of us got it in the right order.

She let us know the heart has an organ known as the eye, known for eternity as a poem for love.

For love she would split open your proverbs, lift you by the hands and teach you to walk.

There is no alien corn where she walks, all mothers are sisters, all songs are source, all listen well.

Jesus pursued her as she ran, into our arms she ran, at the finish line that just plain disappeared.

Go to the origin, he told her, go to the heart of the poorest, help him learn a life, be a poem.

Note the flash of light from the underside of a leaf, and do not sully it with a poor human simile.

You are sight, you are what we need to see a world, call it physical if that is enough, call it home.

You are the second person and there is no third, you are a vision we are treated to see, you are we.

Bless you for being here on the margin where we all must live, blessings be upon you for this venture.

The Figure of Onward

He was forever getting drunk and trying to punch out someone in a bar or at a party, especially his real friends.

He hung out with the action painters, no wonder, and you can't figure out why he didn't die at age thirty in a car crash.

At age thirty-seven he tried to punch me out during a party at Jamie Reid's funky apartment, and I could have decked him.

Then he went south and I went east, and I said during all my travels I'll keep an eye out for you.

He was awfully young to be a hero but he used to raise chickens with good blood lines.

He was a New Englander and in his last letter to me he typed out eighteen lines of "Snowbound" by John Greenleaf Whittier.

"And felt the strong pulse throbbing there / Beat with low rhythm our inland air."

Everyone loves his words—curiously, apropos, more accurately, insistent proposal, literally, lovely, I hear, I hear.

He didn't exactly fall off that chair in Prince George, and he wasn't pushed, and he didn't jump, this was poetry.

Poetry and drunkenness, haven't you ever heard of that, where have you been the past three thousand years?

In the courtyard at midnight he stopped and looked at the moon, and then he mounted the steps with happiness, he was there.

Straight Pant Legs

Every time I talked with Louis Dudek I was startled to see that he was as tall as I am, and I have always been a little nervous about writers tall as I am.

Ted Blodgett, John Marshall, Graeme Gibson, these are writers taller than I am, okay, but Louis was from Montreal, they are usually short in Montreal.

They are usually Jewish in Montreal, and Louis only looked kind of a little European, but not really Jewish except when he was one of the ten Jewish poets at Louis Kearns's *bris*.

The other thing Louis Dudek was was square, in the good old Canadian sense of square, I mean he said things straight ahead.

He didn't mind it that he was not hip because he did not even know about the concept of hip.

Now, I always wanted to appear hip, but I can tell you, in 1958 Louis Dudek and Irving Layton and Raymond Souster were my Canadian heroes.

Nobody in their generation in Canada was hip. Not until Leonard Cohen, and then not really a lot till Victor Coleman.

Leonard Cohen was the young guy around Irving Layton, and Victor Coleman was the young guy around Raymond Souster.

If I had been living in Montreal I would have been the young guy around Louis Dudek, and standing straight as I could and also hip.

Raymond Souster wanted everyone to read William Carlos Williams, Louis Dudek wanted everyone to read Ezra Pound, and Irving Layton wanted everyone to read Irving Layton.

Louis went to a lot of work and dreamed a long dream to write those long poems, and no one reads them, Canadians prefer little poems like candies.

He was extremely earnest, that is the right word, extremely earnest, and he had a great admiration for print, and I always wondered whether he really knew where the young were.

Long Night Blaze

When he wore that hat we called him Irving the Greek, a
present participle in the Mediterranean.

They named gas stations after him all over the Maritimes,
high octane poetry at the pump, free air.

He was a short guy with a broken nose, some muse hit him
with her knee early in life.

A good thing—poems came pouring out, songs of himself,
quotations from some Solomon heaven.

He arrived just in time, shouted down law-dee-daw petit
point afternoon verse, faint sighs in clean Westmount.

When he wasn't Irving he was teaching, instructing his
charges to shut up and listen, grab every trout that swims by.

"Brain, heart, valour, lust, / Thought itself fall into dust," he
said, perched on a rooster's back.

But dust is earth we grow from, dirt under fingernails,
fingers grasping ballpoint pens, Irving living again.

He came naked and circumcised into this world; now he's
naked and hairy in a new one, looking for an editor.

Tomorrow he'll be wrestling an angel, winner gets top
billing and all eternity to read his words from the flame.

Butterfly Pillar

She had a round white face surrounded by a dark musical Greek restaurant.

Joe Rosenblatt followed her all over town with his galoshes unbuckled.

She otherwise undid our compositional hearts with her sweet brave ambition and little nose.

You couldn't see her famous eyes when she was working the pedals of her black bike.

Any poem about Gwen goes on and on, as if it were walking through sawdust.

She recited her poems with no book in her hand, no glasses on her face.

Tom Marshall pined for her and Elizabeth Taylor, who emulated her Egyptian eyes.

Her voice when she recited was the voice of a little girl or a retired schoolteacher.

Time treated her like a drunken clock headed for a hangover in eternity.

They all loved her, they all loved her, and did I love her? Sure, I loved her.

Up off the Floor

First he had a lip for a trumpet, brass boy, Kampus King, now he's got grandchildren from all over, sing it.

Wing it, wait for no syntax, walk forward into visible breath, he says I have been here on this high terrain.

Been here all along, somehow celestial as we said in school, a few of us, readers where the others were right as rain.

Where rime, if you fall on it, is accidental, a name for music, what you do with it, that is blow your inside out.

Learn later old Coleridge did it sooner, what instrument, what trans-creation did he bring to bear?

What whistle keeps the big shaggy animals away, young man with a horn, daughters too old to be mothers.

Air too cold to pucker, give me a kiss, Pauline, he's known her since her house was made of stones, she skis.

She breaks her bones, she skis again, that's the way she is, he has a lot of brass, lot of wind, some Chinese in him, a name.

To breathe normally, as they say after takeoff, count the continents as your own, Frederic, Wah hah hah hah, it happened.

Life *is* interesting, and poetry made it that way, and a B-flat cornet made the poetry, and you *do* walk differently on a slope in the Kootenays.

Walking hand in hand
with a monkey leaving home
comes just before verse.

Vermeer's Light

Vermeer's light
on a chicken's head
puts the lie to form,

allows his love
for content

or not.

Whatever You Do

Whatever you do, do not

slam the year open with a bang,

waken the child

sleeping under that tree

into terror, that tree

dying in our back yard,

birds lining up to mourn. You

wanted a cheer for new

lang syne? Have you looked at the under

cutting of the North Shore mountains,

have you heard four-wheel drives

passing your sweet coupé

on the rain slick of Burrard?

Let that babe sleep, let

chainsaw rest in watershed,

tell politico it's all right to be short,

tell him forget auld acquaintance,

have a look at this

sleeper 'neath our tree,

wake this sweet bairn if need be

with a cup of kindness, two handles,

show this dear drowsy head

the homemade paper you're holding—

it's the deed, hand it to that kid,

say keep this here, don't

let them take it anywhere, south or up the tower.

That's right, compañero, and say, that wee critter

looks powerful like you, you

must be proud, lucky dad.

As an earthquake rocks a corpse

in its coffin in the clay

so are you rocked in your desire,

so do you meet a living January,

so does Nature, call her that again,

depend on your doting, how we have

reversed our lot, oh Death

we address not, but list with new ear

to the Spirit herself utter her fear

of us.

    Look, we've wakened the child, how

can we teach her be not us,

how give her power and sweetness,

and tell her what acquaintance should

be forgot?

        Spread a rictus along your jaw,

dad, help raise a whoop and pretend

this will one day all be hers,

poor orphan, whose face even now

is shaded by that dead branch.

Have You Heard

Have you heard a chainsaw?

It sounds as if
            it will not stop.

I will stop.

I grew here surrounded.

Now they are nearly all
            gone where I will go.

They heard it and wrote books
made of paper near the ocean
in the twilight
in December
at a discount
on a budget
in the gloaming
in an eye blink
it was over.

We Are

We are,
this world and its neighbours,
the joining of God's ejaculate
and his wife's nurture.

She Carries

She carries my chair,
she carries my walker,
she carries my commode,
she drops my heart
      so hard it breaks into
      a hundred pieces

and they all follow her,
in love like Jupiter in orbit.
      She hands me
      my crutches. I carry
my soul to her and say
      here, that's all
      I got to say.

Now, at last, she says,
      you have a good
      attitude.

Q & A

Where are the snows of yesteryear?

Don't bother looking around.
Either they have long melted into the air
that fish glide through,
or they are heaped behind your heart
where no one will ever see them.

Who killed Cock Robin?

I'd guess someone with snow
heaped behind his heart. Robin
offered love and wisdom, two things
people with a frozen chest cannot
abide. Forget yesteryear, remember
last night.

What is the meaning of life?

The condition or attribute of living
or being alive; animate existence.
Opposed to *death*. Whoever killed
Cock Robin holds the key to that
mystery. You do not, no more than
do those fish below the pier.

Why do we have to die?

That is not even a mystery,
we say at first, until someone

asks us to define all our terms, such as
heart-beat. Some people say we die
to make room for strangers, does that
answer your question, stranger?

Is it nothing to you?

Nothing, I agree, is sacred, zero
is to be worshipped, there is nothing
in the heart, next to nothing in the
imperfect life. Caring is another thing,
there is nothing behind true caring.

Are you kidding?

Our subject here is death. That and life.
Do you think I would kid you about that?
You who do not even know the whereabouts
of the snows of yesteryear? You innocent!
When I am kidding about death and life
you will be the first to know. Make that
the last.

What's the difference?

When I took on the job of answerman,
I planned to reply:
Wouldn't you like to know?

How should I know?
That's for me to know and you to find out.
Search me.
If I told you, we'd both know.

What's the score?

All I can tell you, little fish,
is that you are not winning. Your chance of winning
is zero. Follow your heart if you like—
it's not going anywhere. The game, if that's
what it is, is as good as over. You don't want
to know the score.

What's for dinner?

It all depends. If a certain guest shows up,
you are for dinner. If not, we are serving heart.

Why me?

Do you believe in a Supreme Deity?
He hates you like the dickens.
He hates you so much that whenever you are around
he likes to kid about death and life.
If you weren't so tied up with the meaning of life
you might have learned something. Where's
your sense of humour?

How—?

Whoops, I asked a question there.
I'm not supposed to ask the questions around here.
I don't give a shit where the snows of yesteryear
might be. Sorry, you were saying—?
Whoops, that was a question mark, eh?
Whoops!

Are you finished?

Ask your heart. Look behind your heart
where the cold is, ask the dinner guest,
ask your Supreme Deity. You don't even
know who I am. Why are you asking me
all these questions? Whoops, there I go again.

Where are you going?

If I knew, I wouldn't tell you, stranger.
Ask around, somebody ought to know,
don't you think?

Pages Move

Yes, there were people hid books
behind false walls, pages closed on words

whose worth measured even with
death, the prize for their discovery.

These people are heroic, some police
terrorizing mortals for their pleasure

at the pleasure of religion. People
of the Book punish the book. It is writ

they shalt not read. Demonic
priests will read for you, lose

their hearts for your appetite. The moving
finger writes and you are told

move on! How impressive the moveable type
of some fake martyr's soul. Inside

those walls the pages move, while
some illiterate ruler bequeaths death

to a writer spread thin as scripture.
What deep, deep faith, what urge

brings mortal to copy this dictation,
what answering hunger to fix

those lovely markings to live
longer than a single life brought to the gibbet.

Ask a Stupid Question

"How do I love thee?"

You talking to me, Lady?

   "What men or gods are these? What maidens loth?
  What mad pursuit? What struggle to escape?
   What pipes and timbrels? What wild ecstasy?"

Lady, that's just some old pot.

"A child said What is the grass?"

I hope you pointed at the green stuff.

"Shall I compare thee to a summer's day?"

Oh, yeah, that's just what I need. I'm hot and dry and long.

"If you were going to get a pet
  what kind of animal would you get?"

Maybe a big dog, to keep strangers away, stranger.

"If Winter comes, can Spring be far behind?"

I'd guess about three months.

"Shall I part my hair behind? Do I dare to eat a peach?"

Hey, you can part your *bare* behind. You can eat a watermelon, for all
I care.

"And you, Garcia Lorca, what were you doing down by the
watermelons?"

Heh heh heh heh heh.

"What immortal hand or eye,
        Could frame thy fearful symmetry?"

You think *that's* scary? You should see my bare behind!

"How can we know the dancer from the dance?"

Well, you see, the babe with the tutu on: she's the dancer. That stuff she's doing? That's the dance. Jesus, Lady, don't you know anything?

She Walks

She walks *with* me
as she walked *for* me,

a wraith made of flesh
solid on her feet.

So faithful, I walk
with her, keeping

up, more or less,
on my own.

She stands and waits
I believe, full

in her belief that I,
that is I, am here *beside*.

Central Canadian Verse

Back in Ontario, waiting for a melt,
he is, he thinks, at last him-
self, at last the spine he stood on, the bone
encased matter of dreams or at least curious picking
fingers. Has he written
about this, is it entering at the pre-cortex or forehead,
what it is they wanted him to say
thirty-five years ago, when even
the sides of your trousers had a gleam
that would go away when you got your first
real accolades. Waiting for a melt
as if he were some cigarette-chewing Purdy in a cottage
with holes in the walls. He is happy enough, he is older than need be,
he is thankful for small pleasures, he is waiting for one
called water running out
from under the snow.

Lost in the Library

I'm lost in the library,
stranded in the stacks.

I'm a standing huckleberry
wearing stainèd slacks.

I'm simply ordinary
and I'm loaded down with facts,

looking for myself
on the shelf.

I'm looking at my name
on a couple dozen spines.

I'm contemplating fame
in a field that's full of mines.

I'm dressed up for the game
and I'm sweating out some lines,

knocking off a poem
far from home.

A poet's true ambition
is to fiddle with a muse.

And if he goes fishin'
he'll be fishin' for the blues.

But if he stops wishin'
he'll be walkin' with no shoes,

walkin' down the street
iambic feet.

2.

I'm a wreck
in the bibliothèque.

I've got time,
I've got rime,

I've got a really dirty neck.

I can't write my way
out of a wet paper Dewey decimal.

Right now my skill
and most of my will

are infinitesimal.

I'm lost in the library,
feel like a book,
can't find my nook,

you dig? I'm thinking
they got me surrounded.

What am I doing here?
They're going to cross me off their
list in the library.

                    I'm hounded.
I'm a lost dog, you dig?

3.

See what I'm saying?
That muse, she isn't loosed
in any library,
not even a museum.

No, sir, you see 'em in the forest
where the trees ain't pulp
yet and paper ain't wet yet
and no one has to punch
any clock you can set yet.

I mean, look in here,
I'll never last in the library,
meanin' those books can stay,
they're not me, I'm on the high prairie
where muses have nowhere to hide,
and trees have to grow inside.

4.

At least in the library
food is not allowed.

Lunch was temporary,
poetry is proud.

Some of it is scary,
some of it is loud.

Give your empty belly
back to Shelley.

There's lust in the library,
don't get me wrong.

There's a taste for huckleberry,
hunger for a song.

It ain't all funerary,
but it ain't where I belong.

I've got no sonnet—
just a bee in my bonnet.

Opening Day

for George Stanley

On opening day
        you can open your stance,
        you can open a book,

take a good look, yeah,
        take a liking, like
        to a Viking.

Take a swing at a thing
        like a sinker, ahuh,
        be a thinker,

think of getting down to second,
        take a second.
        take a look.
        take a lead-off,
        read a book.

Rounding third, like a bird,
        read the sign
        from your coach,
        your approach

        to the plate,
        isn't late,
        isn't great,
        but okay, okay, okay,

okay, you're safe,
        safe at home,

read a poem,
read *this* poem,

read about base,
read about ball,
read about baseball.

I mean don't delay it.
Get down and play it.

Perseverance

When your snoring
    reaches level two
I place my cool foot
    on your calf.

It is quiet at once
    till I beckon sleep
and you recommence your comment.
    Then I smile for your perseverance.

His Friend Waiting

His friend waiting at the temple, bright
rabbits squash so easily underfoot, he
wore the wrong clothes all week, religion
not his strong suit, trees too dark

in his memory. At the temple, thought
entered his head because he was exhausted.
His friend was a beautiful woman
with black hair and no talent for yodelling.

No talent for the Alpine sort of yodelling
high in valleys you never heard of,
you in your favourite sweater and cap
listening to Lisa's horribly loud earth machines

and promising to stop eating meat, meat
and small British automobiles, such
biography as we seldom see. His friend
grates out a sentence, this is all so

regular, who brought us here, what
animal do I catch faint odour of
among those Alpine trees, sorry little
bits of nature, no insult to the temple

nor even its door—that humans should have
the notion of egress, nothing further from
their minds than large birds, wings pointing
left and right. Your knee, he said, is

cute as can be, peeking from the rent
in your coveralls' leg. I looked and found

a line twigged from Randall Jarrell,
in the land of spelling, far behind the comet's

tail, in the daze of morning you were not
ready for.

A Small Hand

There is a small hand in the purple

Really, I saw this just before All Saints Day

I don't care whether I get Coke or Pepsi

Late at night reading the sky for pins

My father did this, his occupation showing

Thumb nails together staying out of Hell

So I will never visit there again

That path winding when it did not need to

West Side Haiku

Your trees

    Have taken on

The shapes you dreamed.

    Two books on back seat.

Dog leaves kennel, enters car,

    pees on literature

Traffic light green

    against blue sky

sticky, sticky air

Squirrel tries to climb fence

     carries eight nuts

and no laugh track

Moth falls out of bathmat

     What a world

without safety

High-heels at the ballpark

     has a ticket

isn't in a hurry to sit down

Grandma in her grave

     lies grinning

up at heaven.

Bass guitar

booms through the woodwork

     Hope crumbles away

Fred thinks his memory

     beats mine just because it's

more like what happened.

She Gazes

She gazes into her world, a
screen of lives she woman-
ipulates, until star slips into
place. "Sorry I'm late,"

                              but
already she is calming the ocean
near an uncle's heart, easing
a death in the family.

                    At
the table her laptop knows no
lap, the edge of that ocean
is a mind my darling handles

as if juggling puppies, as if gods
joined her for lunch. She gazes
into a universe deep inside
that screen, and I know

my coming year is form-
ulated, happy as mathematics
can be, and she says there is
nothing to it, meaning
everything.

Heap o' Trouble

I'm in big trouble
'cause I don't hip the hop.
I'm working on a sonnet
and I can't seem to stop.
I gotta write it down
like a pail and a mop,
gotta keep my eye out
for the spoken word cop.

Them police
are after my valise.
It's full of poems,
poems on paper,
poems in books,
poems full of grammar
gonna send me to the slammer.

2.

I'm in a heap o' trouble
'cause I just don't slam.
I'm workin' on a lyric
gonna get me in a jam.
I left my banjo
down in Alabam.

I can't recite it,
so you can just bite it.
Here, let me ignite it,
you can dance to the flame.

I'm lame.
I'm game.
I'm just about ready to use a new name.

Call me D. J. Square.

3.

I'm on the bubble
'cause I don't perform.
I'm working on an epic
and I'm riding out the storm.
I love authority.
I want to be the norm.
I want to be asleep
in an academic dorm.

I don't hate my parents.
I don't hate my teachers.
I don't hate the cops,
and I can stand the preachers.

I'm D. J. Square.
I want to be fair.
I want you to like me
for my tidy hair.

I want you to know, this ain't no caper.
I sit right down
and I write on paper.

I'm D. J. Square,
the paperboy.

Cates Park and Later That Night

There were pine cones on the beach
and rocks an inch below the surface.
Every step I took hurt more
than those I took long years before.
I watched the Vietnamese play volleyball
and thought of David W. McFadden because
I often put him into a poem, where
he is happier than he is at home
with his toaster. The person I live with
is far prettier than the Toronto poet.
I go for walks with her and Malcolm Lowry,
that other writer of sonnets, an Englishman
through and through, gin drinker, precious accent,
bare chest in the colony, ear of an angel
nearby. Pine cones black on the beach, or
so the light makes them look. She is sitting
beside me now, blessed order in the happenstance
of my late years. Below the surface is where
I've never been, or so I say. I learned to swim
by employing my arms like fins underwater,
or levers, some kind of angelic flesh, hard
bone, tested joint. The Vietnamese
turn little pieces of meat on a barbecue
in the sunlight, no visible flame, no occidental
purpose. Everyone comes to this park
but I, who might if he could, re-
enter old-fashioned human procedure, this
retired poet, his country's uncomplaining ward.

A Riopelle Exhibit

How could you not
love that thick paint

that Quebec man so brave
you have tears in your eyes

sixty years after he
laid his knife, in another

country, here we go, tears
rimming your eyeballs

vision falling away except
when he, moments like this

pays the big money, a life
with *richesse* in it, time

to time, thick paint
at the heart of thinking.

She Drives

She drives the car, and this
is her theory—get into the left lane
and floor it.

        Sometimes my chair
was in the trunk, sometimes
I just want to hear poetry
on the radio, poetry from a mouth
        of a friend who just will not
shut up.

        She never curses other drivers,
those people the rest of us call
        assholes.

She drives the city, and now
        she knows it, right lane or left,
she drives the car
        while the choir ascends
and the dog makes carcinogenic smells
        in the rear seat.

She's a good driver, another reason
        to live with her, who knows
how to unfold that chair
        as if it were a heart
and I need a new one.

        They did my right eye that way
so I can see her,
        eyes intent on the QEW

and its huge turning wheels,
       its poet below the underpass,
its voice a pile-up in the snow.

      She drives the Volvo in Oklahoma
and we never get pulled over,
       another reason to put my hand
       on her right knee
       and to say
       thanks for the lift.

Rewriting My Grandfather

In *Survival*, her famous "thematic guide to Canadian literature," Margaret Atwood had quite a bit to say about grandfathers. For example: "Grandfathers may be treated as isolated subjects in poems, and such poems emphasize most often their negative strengths, the fervour with which they disapprove and repress … they rule, or attempt to rule, their children with a rod of iron. They are patriarchs." This is what she said about what I wrote about my grandfather: "The grandfather as rigid and threatening icon, self-proclaimed embodiment of morality and the Calvinist Will of God, is glimpsed in full flower." Putting aside the question of how all that stuff can be a flower, I have to say that I thought my grandfather came off a little better than that in my poem. Here is how it goes, according to all the textbooks I have seen:

Grandfather
            Jabez Harry Bowering
strode across the Canadian prairie
hacking down trees
                    & building churches
delivering personal baptist sermons in them
leading Holy holy holy lord god almighty songs in them
red haired man squared off in the pulpit
reading Saul on the road to Damascus at them

Left home
            big walled Bristol town
at age eight
                to make a living
buried his stubby fingers in root snarled earth
for a suit of clothes & seven hundred gruelly meals a year

taking an anabaptist cane across the back every day
for four years till he was whipt out of England

Twelve years old
                    & across the ocean alone
to apocalyptic Canada
                        Ontario of bone bending labour
six years on the road to Damascus till his eyes were blinded
with the blast of Christ & he wandered west
to Brandon among wheat kings & heathen Saturday nights
young red haired Bristol boy shovelling coal
in the basement of Brandon College five in the morning

Then built his first wooden church & married
a sick girl who bore two live children & died
leaving several pitiful letters & the Manitoba night

He moved west with another wife & built children & churches
Saskatchewan Alberta British Columbia Holy holy holy
lord god almighty
                        struck his laboured bones with pain
& left him a postmaster prodding grandchildren with crutches
another dead wife & a glass bowl of photographs
& holy books unopened save the bible by the bed

Till he died the day before his eighty-fifth birthday
in a Catholic hospital of sheets white as his hair

I never thought getting tickled with the end of a crutch was all that
threatening.

I wrote that poem when I was twenty-six. Years later I found the hasty
autobiography my grandfather wrote in his room at the back of our house
in Oliver. Here is his last paragraph: "In Feb 1953 I sold the house in

Penticton and Ewart made some changes in his house so that I could move to Oliver and live with them and I shall stay with them until I am called to the Home Beyond and my body is placed beside my beloved Wife Clara. Rev. 22-20. Surely I come quickly. Amen, Even so come Lord Jesus."

There are some discrepancies between his own handwritten life account and the poem I wrote at age twenty-six. I will tell the story of the birth of that poem.

Recently I was looking through my diary as I seldom do, and fell upon early October of 1962. U.S. president Kennedy would be starting the Cuban missile crisis in three weeks. The Berlin Wall had been up for a year. Here's what I saw in my diary: the handwriting of my oldest friend, Will Trump, who was, in 1962, my roommate. Riffling a few pages, I came upon some awkward lettering done by my left hand.

Early in the morning of September 30, 1962, I had broken my right hand. I did this by punching a concrete wall as hard as I could. The concrete wall had burlap pasted to it. I thought the wall was made of plaster. In recent times I had taken to punching plaster walls as an expression of my frustration with the changeable affection of my beautiful girlfriend Angela Luoma. I was taking some chance, I thought, that my fist would strike a plaster wall just where there was a two-by-four stud, rather than dramatically crashing through plaster. So far I hadn't hit a stud—or a girlfriend, ever.

The concrete wall was in the staircase of the hipster apartment of poet Jamie Reid and film-maker Sam Perry, overlooking the train tracks along the side of Coal Harbour. In the summer of 1963, Red Lane would do a poetry reading while standing on top of someone's Pontiac in the overgrown yard back of this apartment. Sometimes we would frisbee Jamie's Thelonious Monk records from the balcony, trying to reach the salt water past the CPR tracks.

The reason that I punched the wall was, I think, Angela Luoma's suggestion that we let our relationship go. For a young man the worst thing to see is a loved one with someone else, and that starts with a loved one's breaking a relationship. It makes you want to hit a wall. We had been together, more or less, for a year. I had been punching walls for a month or so.

But this concrete punch seemed to do the job. Angela Luoma and I wound up sleeping together at my rickety second-storey place overlooking False Creek. I had to keep my hand on the pillow above her head. In the morning my hand had grown to be about the size of her head. We went down to St. Paul's Hospital on Burrard Street, and Angela Luoma sat on a bus stop bench across from the hospital while the doctors and nurses put me into a daze and fixed my hand. I remember a needle going in between bones. I remember waking up in an empty operating room with faint light coming from concave lamps.

They put a plaster cast on my hand and wrist and forearm, and I hated it. It was as hard as concrete. It held some of my fingers straight and some of them crooked. I went around sniffing at it—the odour was really something, irresistible. When you have a heavy cast on your hand you are always banging it into door frames and furniture. I was a teaching assistant at UBC. Eighteen-year-olds helped me gather my notes after class.

Meanwhile, I was learning how to write poems and, more important, poetics, mainly domestic versions of William Carlos Williams and Charles Olson. I sat coolly and cared for the syllable. I got over an unfortunate weakness for jazzy rhetoric.

I was a journalist, too, don't forget. I took Angela Luoma to hear Cannonball Adderley's sestet with Yusef Lateef, because I had to review the music for the *Ubyssey* critics' pages. I took notes with my left hand and tried to hold my cigarette with the two straight fingers sticking out of the redolent cast.

But for some reason I came home by myself on the night of October 6. I had probably gone on one of my old-time pub crawls, or a shortened version that did not carry me as far east as the Princeton Hotel. I do, despite the fact that I was too drunk to drive a 1954 Austin, remember trying to get into my linoleumated False Creek digs that night. It was dark. It was raining a straight-down rain. I was carrying twelve bottles of Old Style Pilsner hanging from my two fingers, now as bent as the others. I could not find my front door key. I looked through every pocket, as one will do, three times, with my left hand.

Maybe Will was home. It was about three in the morning, if you can call anything morning above the False Creek warehouses in the rain. Will's girlfriend had to work weekends. He was probably sleeping in their little front room. I could throw a stone that high with my left hand, I told myself, but things are different in the rain when you're between drunk and hungover. The streets are really steep above False Creek, so a second-storey window is pretty high. I started pegging little stones. They got harder and harder to find. I had to keep walking to the streetlight at the corner. Some rattled down the bent creosote shingles below our windows. Some hit nothing but trees and automobiles. But some snapped on a windowpane.

You know what a stone against your windowpane sounds like when you're inside—it's really loud. Especially at three in the morning. But I looked at the dark window for Will's scruffle-haired head, in vain. I would have to use the so-called fire escape—a ladder nailed to the side of the house. If it were possible to get two storeys up on that ladder, I would find a little flat roof covered with warped asphalt shingles outside our little kitchen window. This was the window favoured by two cats we called Meredith and Phyllis.

I did not think that I could make it up that ladder with its rungs so close to the ugly green wall (black wall now in the 3:30 a.m. rain). It was raining persistently, and my eyeglasses were opaque with rain. I was still drunk, or angry enough to make up for whatever sobering I had suffered. I was carrying a dozen Pils. I thought of drinking a couple to lighten the load, but

I could not think of a way to open them. I had to decide what to do with the two bent fingers protruding from the wet and soiled cast around my aching hand. Should I hang the case of beer from them, or use them to support my hundred and eighty pounds (counting the beer)? And how would I reach for the next rung without falling? How do I get into these situations, I asked, as usual.

Now I am trying to remember how I got up there, and I simply cannot, can hardly believe that I did. Getting the kitchen window open was little problem—it stuck and rattled, but the sill was rotted like a rain forest floor, and it would always open eventually.

I got in. Then I put the case of beer into the refrigerator, moving some sushi to make room. I snapped on the kitchen light and looked into the front room, where I saw Will's puzzling shape under a dark blanket. There were no blinds on any of our windows in any of our three rooms. Feeble light fell out of the rainy sky. Dawn would be late and grey.

"I'm home safe and sound," I said quietly.

"Jeeze, Cap'n," he said. "That horrible kid upstairs has been dropping marbles on the floor and out their window on that little roof. What time is it? How do I get any sleep around here?"

I closed the door to the front room.

Then, with my soaked hair on my forehead, I sat down at the kitchen table and wrote my poem "Grandfather." I have not lately seen the manuscript, so I don't know whether I wrote it with my left hand or the aching fingers sticking out from my smelly cast. Then I went to my bed in the side room.

2.

When I got up that afternoon it had stopped raining. Will was gone, probably to get sushi at his girlfriend's. Meredith and Phyllis were at the window. I let them in and gave them some of the oldest raw fish and rice. Outside every piece of nature and rotted fence was silver. There was almost a whole cup of coffee in the pot on the leaking gas stove. I had a bad pain right back of my forehead. I was still emotional but prepared to forgive Will when he blundered through the door.

We went through our usual comic routine, and then he told me that my grandfather poem was the best thing I'd ever written. He had known my grandfather, an old man with bad feet and a British vocabulary.

"What are you talking about?" I inquired. "This thing ignores or violates all the poetic principles that I have been working out these last two years."

"It's really good," he said.

Maybe it is, I thought.

"No, it's all that's wrong with poetry," I said.

Will was studying Japanese. He didn't know anything about poetics.

Still, I published the poem in *Tish 14*, along with a review of Jack Kerouac's *Big Sur*, a book that ends with a long poem a lot different from my short one. "Grandfather" would show up in my first book in 1964, and would appear in all my selected volumes, I think. And it would show up in lots and lots of anthologies, including all those anthologies created for colleges and high schools. It's a "teachable poem," I guess, and thus confirms the reservations I expressed about it when it was less than one day old. Those editors must have agreed with my roommate.

I guess all the poets in Canada were writing poems about their grandfathers in those days. At least the male poets were. I don't remember all that many grandmother poems, although I wrote one that didn't get into the anthologies. Grandfather poems were good for the thematic nationalists of the nineteen sixties and seventies, and were probably good for their successors, the identity post-colonialists of the nineteen nineties. Those old relatives got called things like "prairie patriarchs." They were pioneers of a "national literature" or something like that. They were examples used in essays that employed the adjective "cultural."

But we are living in a new century now, free to talk about how poems are actually written, rather than about what they are used for by their readers from time to time.

Part of the reason that my "Grandfather" was so rhetorical is that my grandfather (he was never called "Jabez" in the family) was a circuit rider in Manitoba and Alberta. I never heard him preach, but I wanted some Baptist noise in the poem. Besides, I was wet and drunkish, and my hand was killing me.

I never even went to church with him. When my grandmother was alive I went with her to the Baptist church in West Summerland, B.C. At home in Oliver, B.C. I went to Sunday school in the United Church. There was no Baptist church in Oliver. In West Summerland with my grandmother I heard the choir and everyone else singing "Holy holy holy, Lord God Almighty." It seemed to bulge the walls a little. The song ended "God in three persons, blessed Trinity." I didn't have a clue what that meant, but it sounded great, and I figured that that's why you would sing "holy" three times. I also knew that the line wouldn't have worked with two of them or four of them. My grandmother did not know that she was taking me to a poetry lesson.

I remember two reading experiences with her. She once disapproved of a book I was reading: *The Gashouse Gang*. She had no idea that it was about the St. Louis Cardinals of the thirties. The other time had to do with her favourite comic strip, *Orphan Annie*. She would read it out loud to me. When the gangsters said "yeah," she read it as "yea." I expected a "verily." I never had the nerve to ask her how she understood that narrative.

3.

There came a time when Allen Ginsberg did not want to read "Howl" to audiences any more, and I know my own little version of what he meant. After a while I would not read my grandfather poem, despite its rhetorical nature, or because of it. Or because, despite the anthologies, I did not relish being a one-trick peony.

Besides, it became embarrassing to recite the errors in the poem, or warn about them before reading it. If you understand poems as linguistic events, they don't have errors in them, but if you read the short handwritten autobiography my grandfather wrote in his last days, you would know that the poem could use a little revision. (As you will see, it would get some, but not because of the errors.)

For one thing, the child who would become my grand-dad did not take an Anabaptist cane across his back every day. I don't think that I even knew what an Anabaptist was when I angrily wrote the poem. According to my grand-dad's autobiography, he was a normal Church of England orphan. In fact, his sister would become a Church of England nun. He became a Baptist (not an Anabaptist) when he found out that he had lost an argument about religion with the farm couple who employed him as an (almost) indentured labourer in Manitoba. He converted, and soon decided to go to divinity school and become a Baptist preacher. So my father's father was not an Anabaptist, but my mother's mother was. Born in Michigan, she was a Mennonite girl, whose family had moved from Oregon to Alberta, where she and her sister married Baptist brothers who had moved there from the Ozarks.

When my grand-dad and his brother came from England to Canada, they came first to Quebec, not to the Ontario of the poem; and when my preacher grandfather moved from Manitoba to Alberta it was not via Saskatchewan that he travelled, but rather through Minnesota, where he was a circuit rider north of Minneapolis. He was all set to take employment in Idaho, when the church asked him to go to work south of Edmonton, where the Lutherans were snapping up too many of the available young believers.

But that's just political geography. He wound up living with my parents after his second wife Clara died, my father Ewart being the dutiful son, I guess. We built another addition to the house. I got my middle name from my grand-dad, as did my father. As for the Catholic hospital in Oliver, B.C., it was the only hospital between Penticton and the border. It was a block from our house. My father was the most energetic organizer in the creation of the new secular hospital. A couple of years ago the beautiful old one was torn down to make room for condominiums. My grandfather took classical languages at divinity school, but he never heard that word.

4.

Still I was not finished with that poem. Every time an anthology comes out, it has "Grandfather" in it. The editors of anthologies, especially those made for universities and high schools, read earlier anthologies for their material. Thus a poem I wrote while wet and pissed off at age twenty-six appears in Gary Geddes's latest, *15 Canadian Poets X 3*, just as I am ending my career as an English professor who never taught that poem in forty years. For years I claimed that I made more from the poem than my grandfather made as a circuit rider around Pilot Mound and Wetaskiwin.

Often, over those years, I have thought of ways in which I could escape that poem, or murder it. I will not dwell on the fact that it has been a sturdy little money-maker. But I found out that an eraser will not work. Just recently I thought of the opposite: I could write it over, or more aptly, over-write it. This time I looked for my inspiration not to a case of B.C. beer, but Oulipo.

I was introduced to Oulipo a few decades ago by my old linguistics teacher Ron Baker. "Oulipo" is an acronym for *Ouvroir de Littérature Potentielle*, a group workshop for writers and mathematicians that has been producing peculiar texts since 1960. Applying artificial restrictions to the making of texts, they produce such oddities as George Perec's famous *La disparition*, a novel that eschews the most common letter in the French language, while telling the story of the disappearance of its protagonist, a man whose name is Vowl, missing a vowel. So it goes. When I published the first portion of this present memoir/essay, I titled it "How I Wrote One of My Poems," a self-important reference to a book called *Comment j'ai écrit certains de mes livres* by Raymond Roussel, godfather of Oulipo. Oulipo's workshop experiments were published and described, and their methods were given interesting names. *La disparition* is an example of a "lipogram," a work with something absent. Lipo is of course the last part of Oulipo. But it is also the first part of liposuction.

In my prose and poetry I have often employed constraints, or "baffles," as I used to call them. Once I travelled around the world, writing a spy novel that had to take place in whatever city I was in at the time, in whatever neighbourhood of that city I was in. But it was also, this novel, a translation of the ancient Greek philosopher Heraclitus's *fragments* as we have them. There were some other constraints that I will not mention now. But I will mention the delight that can come to the writer when he works within such constraints. Where else, in 1985, should a spy novel end up but in Berlin, with its cold war wall?

Heraclitus's most famous fragment says that you cannot step into the same river twice. Probably the second-most-famous is this: "The way up is the way down." When I was living in Berlin in 1985 there were three ways to cross over into East Berlin—the subway, the elevated train or Checkpoint Charlie. The East German authorities had a rule: you had to go back to West Berlin by the same way you had used to go east. I can assure you that compositional constraints lead to plot development.

All right. If you can ravel a spy novel this way, I reasoned with myself, you can certainly unravel a grandfather poem. So my project began; and now I will offer you some of the results. Some experiments, of course, work, some do not. Others will take time. I hope that the last one I offer up might be a surprise as well as an improvement.

(Incidentally, I seem to have lost the manuscript notebook these poems were written in. If anyone finds it, please let me know.)

For my first attempt at roughing up that grandfather poem I employed one of the simplest methods invented by the Oulipo. It is called N+7. First you name the dictionary you are using, and then you remove every noun in the poem, substituting the noun that comes seven nouns later in the dictionary. I used the thick and heavy Random House *Compact Unabridged Dictionary* (the 1996 printing). Here is what it gave me:

GRAND FIR

Grand fir
        Jaddua Herman Bowering
strode over the Canadian prairie dog

hacking off tree ears
                and building churchgoers,
delivering personal Baptist serositis to them,
red-haired management squared off in the pulsar
reading Semachiah on the road-gang to Danielson to them

Left homebuilding
                big walled Bristol town hall
at Agenais
        to make Livingstone,
buried his stubby finger gate in root-cap-snarled earthlight
for a suk of clothes-poles and seven hundred gruelly meander lines year-round,
taking an Anabaptist caner across the back-beat every day-book
for four year-rounds till he was whipped out of Englewood

Twelve year-rounds old
             and across Oceania alone
to apocalyptic Çanakkale,
                Ootacamund of bone-earth-bending labourer,
six year-ends on the road-gang to Danielson till his eye-bolts were blinded

with the blastocyst of Cleopas and he wandered west
to Branson among king clams and heathen Friday night snakes,
young red-haircut Bristol boyfriend shovelling coal-fish
in the basepath of Branson college radio five in the morning line

Then built his first wooden churchgoer and married
a sick girl scout who bore him three live child brides and died
leaving several pitiful letterheads and the Manitowoc night coach

He moved west with another wigeon and built child brides and churchgoers,
Satanta, Albi, Britton, Holy holy holy
lording goddess almighty
                                    struck his laboured bone-earth with painted beauty
and left him a post-nasal drip prodding grandfathers with cruzeiros,
another dead wigeon and a glass bowline of photojournalism
and holy bookcases unopened save the Biblia Pauperum by the bed chair

Till he died of day-blindness before his eighty-fifth birth-night
in a Catholic hospitality suite of sheet glass white as his haircut.

It seemed funny to me, how much the spirit of the original poem remained. But I also loved some of the images that Random House (neat name, eh?) gave me. Imagine my grandfather squared off in the pulsar!

All right. I wanted to get a little further away from the spirit of the original. So I invented my own little procedure. This time I would use the same dictionary, but change both the verbs and the nouns. I would locate the original word and then go five hundred pages forward in the dictionary, finding the word that rested on the appropriate part of the page. If the original word started with a letter near the end of the dictionary, I would keep going, lapping the beginning of the book. Sure enough, the poem became less sensible, more like *avant-garde* Language poetry:

A GLASS FOREARM

Nugacity, Jabez Harry Bowering,
busked across the Canadian trial-run
opening up caricatures
                        and fulfilling hard disks,
jetting personal Ethiopian alburnums in them,
red-opportunitied rodomontade baby-talked in the undoing,
varying Saul in the wet-suit of Damascus to them.

Raised parsimony
                    big walled Bristol canal
at derris eight
                to rive a reign,
gainsaid his stubby military police in whittling arbitrated likelihood
for a bias of hemialgia and seven hundred gruelly sagas a czarina,
bombing a District of Columbia giblet across the enunciation every irrelevance
for four czarinas till he was disinterred out of England.

Twelve czarinas old
                    and across the spiritual bouquet alone
to apocalyptic Canada,
                        Ontario of flotilla-faking put and take,
six czarinas in the wet-suit of Damascus till his maturation was fire-proofed
with the fingerprint of Christ and he contracted west
to Brandon among coup provosts and heathen Saturday slip-covers,
young red-opportunitied Bristol forequarter amusing Heraclitus
in the evolutionary biology of Brandon hill, five in the service station.

Then fulfilled his first wooden hard disk and rucked
a sick non-bank which explored two live hags and kerned,
rainbowing several pitiful ravines and the Manitoba slip-cover.

He shambled west with another anaconda and fulfilled hagiology and hard disks,
Saskatchewan, Alberta, British Columbia, Holy holy holy
repudiation nonsequitor almighty

                                     beefed up his laboured flotilla with submersibles
and raised him a supertitle two-timing nudibranches with innocence,
another dead anaconda and a glass forearm of terms
and holy flumes unopened save the faucet by the extinguisher.

Till he kerned the irrelevance before his eighty-fifth fibrin
in a Catholic Pax Romana of aluminum white as his opportunity.

Imagine, I had now written a poem with words I don't remember the meanings of! But you should see how labour-intensive this kind of poetry is. It is just the opposite of gushing out some lyric about something you had a feeling about that day. And that is, I think, the point.

Speaking of the opposite, here is a piece that you might honestly call work. I took the nouns, verbs and adjectives of the poem and replaced them with their opposites. In the cases of place names, I went to the other side of the map, checking out longitude and latitude:

LOWLY SATAN

Grandson
        George Harry Bowering
crept over the Siberian mountains,
patching up trees
                and demolishing dens of iniquity,
receiving impersonal Catholic pornography outside them,
following Unholy unholy unholy peasant Satan weakling prose outside them,
blue-haired woman sideways outside the last pew
writing Saul off the road to Honolulu away from them.

Came away
             to small undefended Aleutian isle
at age sixty-three
             to bum around,
exhumed his long toes from sliding sand
to remain naked and eat extravagantly all year,
removing an Orthodox comforter from his chest every night
for four years till he was sucked into Dutch Harbor.

Sixty-seven years old
             and onto the continent in a herd
from Edenic west central Siberia,
             Altais of flesh-straightening ease,
six years off the lane from Honolulu since his vision began
in the dark of demons and he beelined east
to Omsk away from wheat slaves and Christian Sunday mornings,
old white-skinned Aleutian man piling snow
from the attic of Omsk prison house, five in the evening.

Then razed his last stone whorehouse and divorced
a healthy crone who suffered two stillbirths and thrived,
sending scarce ebulliant postcards minus the Siberian daytime.

He stayed east without a single woman and razed whorehouses and parents,
Novosibirsk, Kemerovo, Khakass, Profane profane profane
lowly Satan puny
             embraced his flesh with balm
and employed him as train-robber massaging grandfathers with silk,
no more living mistresses and no wooden knives without decoration,
and nothing profane to read except the Sears catalogue on the floor.

After which he sprang to life following his second childhood
outside a Baptist fort of bricks red as his skin.

But you hear what is happening here. The words change in various ways, but the poem sounds much as it did. It is still more than halfway there. I could have written such stuff soaking wet and drunk at my kitchen table if I had been less guilty of autobiography, or grampabiography, I guess.

So what about, I asked myself, keeping the story and changing the form? How about using one of the oldest methods of *littérature potentielle* that we all know? The one used by Shakespeare, Milton, Wordsworth and Shelley? I am talking about the sonnet, in this case the Shakespearean, or English, sonnet:

DAUGHTERS SECULAR

His father died and left him Bristol's wall,
which at the age of eight he battered through.
He made a living, did not hear a call,
but only felt the cane each morning new.

At twelve he crossed an ocean and a line
to fetch up in the mud of old Quebec.
He bent his back and did not see a sign
but slowly went upon his westward trek.

The Baptist Jesus nabbed him on the plain
and put him in a college, there to learn
the ways of holy rhetoric and pain
and sent him twice to marry and to burn.

He sired daughters secular, and sons,
and died in care of hale and silent nuns.

Maybe if I had stayed home and sober and calmly portrayed my grandfather by way of a Shakespearean sonnet, Margaret Atwood would not have found him to be so "rigid and threatening."

I felt a sense of irony, as I kept coming back to the poem I was trying to get out of my life. There is a similar contradiction in the world of computer word processors: one feels an estrangement as soon as the meat sits down in front of the machine. The word "digital," which used to mean the fingers that we think with, now means something we cannot imagine but which works to build words and pass them on, via satellites high above the earth, or so we are told. Estrangement, but also a kind of intimacy, in which one feels oneself entering, by way of the fingers, the world on the screen or maybe on the other side of it.

Or not.

But the modern poet sits, as I am sitting now, in front of the illuminated screen. I subjected my grandfather poem to some "programs" created by a stranger in an unknown environment.

First, Ms. Jean Baird told me about something called Babel Fish©. It is a computerized translation program, and of course because it is imperfect it interested me. I submitted the poem to a translation into Spanish and back out to English:

EATEN CLOTHES

Grandfather
      Jabez Harry Bowering
walked with big steps through the Canadian prairie

cutting under trees
                     & constructed churches
gave personal sermons of the Baptist in them
the All-powerful songs of God santo santo main santo
of the red gentleman in them
haired the fit man extinguished in Saul reading of the pulpit
in the road to Damascus in them

The great emparadada city
                     left caretaker Bristol
at age eight
           to make a life
buried his dumpy fingers in root grunió earth
for a game of eaten clothes & seven hundred gruelly to the year
that took to a cane from anabaptism through the posterior every day
for four years until they whipped it outside England

Twelve years as an older person
                     and through the ocean
to apocalyptic Canada
                Ontario of the work of boy
of flexion of the bone
                six years in the way to Damascus
until their eyes were only blinded
with the burst of Christ and he vagó to the west
to Brandon between kings of the wheat
& the red young person of the pagan nights of Saturday
haired the boy of Bristol that traspalabra the coal
to the cellar of university five of Brandon in the morning.

Later he constructed his first wood church & married
an ill girl who bore two alive children & at night
died leaving several lamentable letters & Manitoba

He moved to the west with another wife & constructed children
& All-powerful santo santo British santo of the God
of the Mr. of Saskatchewan Alberta Colombia of the churches
pulse his bones worked with pain & to the left
he a postmaster that punctured grandsons with muletas
another dead wife and a bowl of crystal source of photographies
and not opened holy books except the bible by the bed

Until he died the day before his first birthday
Eighty in a catholic hospital the target of the leaves like his hair

Some of it is goofy, all right, but look at some of the things one can gain with a little giving up of control—that wonderfully apt word "emparadada," for example.

So I went with Babel Fish© once more, this time letting it translate my grandpa into French, thence into German, and back to English:

ON THE ROAD

Grandfather
          Jabez Harry Bowering
is the Canadian, the meadow by,
which cut down trees and which
church construction advanced, which
supplied personal Baptistpredigten in them, all
powerful songs of a holy holy holy
main gentleman God in them
red shark-talk square humans on far
in the Saul reading of the desk on the road
in Damas at them

The large city,
                which was immured at the left
Bristolpapierhaus at age eight, in order
to make a life
                thundered their fingers blunted in the root
buried the earth for clothes and sieves one hundred
mahlzeit gruelly per year, which each day
at one anabaptiststock by the back during
four years,
                until he was whipped outside of England.

Twelve years
                and through alone ocean
in apokalyptischen Canada
                        Ontario of the
work, of the children, of the bone curvature
were dazzled six years over the road
in Damas jusqu'in its eyes with the breath
of the Christ, and it has in the torch/flare
west among grain kings and the red young person
shark-talk Saturday heidnische nights
geumherirrt the Bristolpapierjunge, which digs
the coal in the basement of University of five,
of the torch/flare, of the mornings

A builds then its first church from wood
and a girl badly married

It shifted in the west with another wife and children built,
and whole-powerfully sainte holy holy British

of a gentleman God from Saskatchewan
Alberta Colombia von Kirchen struck it with the pain bone
operated has and left,
                    the postmaster
it enkelkinder with sprags to stab,
another dead wife and a dish from glass
of photographs and non-open holy books to save
the bible by the bed.

Until it died on the day before its fifth birthday
eighty in a Catholic hospital
                    of page dummy key as its hair

Now, I thought, we are getting somewhere. But where? This was threatening to make my poetry seem as good as the poetry of Erin Mouré or Fred Wah. I thought briefly of doing this to all my poems, of jumping over the *avant garde* into whatever would happen next. But I am a careful experimenteur at the core. Besides, the grand-dad poem looked as if it would supply me with ideas for years to come.

I tried one more computer program, and I have to say that I am far from the first to do this one. Many poets have produced spell-check poems, letting Microsoft Word's built-in literacy-provider change poems into corporation-approved exercises in composition. It works best, or rather makes the funniest decisions, if you feed in a poem by Milton or Spenser. When I fed "Grandfather" into the spell-check, I got a poem that was very little changed from the "original." It would not repeat the word "Holy," and it would not accept the word "gruelly," supplying, for some reason, maybe because my grandfather went westward, the word "Greeley." It took the "u" out of "labour."

I don't know how long I will go on rewriting and thus trying to extirpate this chestnut. Recently I returned to an old idea. In my earlier days I mingled with Romantic poets, co-writing "Mont Blanc" with Shelley and

"When I Have Fears" with Keats. This time, observing the fact that my grandfather was a preacher, and the other fact that Wordsworth said that he was nature's priest, I decided to mingle my poem and that previous poet laureate's. But first I got out my chopper and cut both poems up. Here's what we got when I remixed:

NATURE'S PREACHER

To apocalyptic Canada, half-extinguished thought,
          Ontario and faint,
Six years on the road to lexity,
with the blast of Christ who lives again:
to Brandon among kingly wheat with the sense of a
young red haired Bristol boy with pleasing thoughts:
in the basement of Brandon is life and food

Then built his first wooden—that time is past,
a sick girl who bore two lives now no more,
leaving several pitiful lectures. Not for this
now, with gleams of snarled earth,
many recognitions, three hundred gruelly meals a year
and somewhat of a sad purpose, back every day.

Picture of the mind roped out of England
while here I stand, not on
present pleasure, but
that in this moment there is the ocean alone.

Grandfather
        Jabez Harry all gone by)
strode across the Canadian, cannot paint,
hacking down trees cataract

and built the tall rock,
delivering personal Baptist and gloomy wood,
leading Holy lord god almighty, then to me
red haired man squared off in love,
reading Saul on the road to deter charm,

                                    any interest.

Left home,
               big walled Bristol wife and built children and churches
for future years. And so Columbia Holy
though changed, no doubt,
I came among these hills; laboured bones with pain,
I bounded o'er the mountain, prodding grandchildren with crutches
of the deep rivers, and the bowl of photographs
wherever nature led: more the bible by the bed
flying from something that
sought the thing, his eighty-fifth birthday.

        He moved west with another white as his hair,
Saskatchewan Alberta British murmur, other gifts,
Lord god almighty loss, I would believe,
               struck, for I have learned
and left him a postmaster as in the hour,
another dead wife and a hearing oftentimes
holy books unopened of humanity,
                    though of ample power.

Till he died the day before, of bone bending labour
in a Catholic hospital on sheets till his eyes were blinded,
and their glad animal move wandered west
to me all in all—I and heathen Saturday nights,
what then I was. The sound of shovelling coal
haunted me like a passion five in the morning.

The mountain and the deep church married
their colours and their children and died,
an appetite, a feeling and the Manitoba night
that had no need of a dare to hope
by thought supplied, nor what I was when first
at age eight when like a roe
      to make a living by the sides
buried stubby fingers in the lonely streams
for a suit of clothes and seven like a man,
taking an Anabaptist cane he dreads,
for four years till he was whipped. For nature then
           my boyish days
twelve years old
        and across sermons in them
unborrowed from the songs in them
and all aching joy the pulpit
and all dizzy rapture, Damascus at them.

Faint I, nor mourn nor own
have followed; for such ring
abundant recompense. Prairie
to look on nature, not churches
of thoughtless youth;
the still, sad music.

Climbing the side of a wet building, looking down the slope of a sunny hill, we start something we cannot finish. I thought that I could. I say the poem ends, and it never does, except for the dead ear that will put such foolishness aside. As Charles Olson said, the only thing we can disavow is disavowal.

Acknowledgements

Above Ground
Backwoods Broadsides
Canadian Literature
Canadian Poetry
The Capilano Review
Dandelion
filling Station
Globe and Mail
Graffito
House Organ
House Press
The IV Lounge Reader, ed. Paul Vermeersch, Insomniac Press
Jacket
Ledger Domain, eds. Charlene Diehl-Jones & Gary Draper, Trout Lily Press
Literary Review of Canada
Nomados
Onsets, ed. Nate Durwood, *The Gig*
Open Letter
Peter F. Yacht Club
Pooka Postcards
Queen Street Quarterly
Rout/e
Tads
Textual Studies in Canada

Vancouver Sun
Victor's Verses, ed. Carol Matthews, Outlaw Editions

"The PGI Golf Tournament Poetic Address and Apology for Same" was spoken at the banquet following the Peter Gzowski Invitational gold tournament for literacy, Vancouver, 1995. A similar travesty was composed for the Victoria tournament in 2003.

A group of theatre students from Brock University performed a dance-theatre version of "The Important Stuff on Granville Island" at the Roselawn Theatre, Port Colborne, Ontario, November 8, 1997.

"Words on Water?" appeared on a brochure, a plaque, etc., at the second annual Campbell River Writers' Festival, 2003.

"Opening Day" appeared in the program for the Canadian Little League championships, August 15–12, 2004.